Hills and Rivers of Guilin

CHINA TRAVEL AND TOURISM PRESS

Chief editor: Yu Tianwei
Deputy chief editor: Zhang Jiaqi
Editors: Meng Zi, Dong Ruicheng, Qi Lijuan
 and Wu Zhaojun
Writer: Liu Shoubao
Translated by: Ji Rongsheng
Designed by: Lü Daqian
Map Cartographer: Teng Yifang
Photos by:
 Wang Wusheng, Bai Liang, Deng Chaoxing, Liu Baoju,
 Zhu Xianmin, Chen Donglin, Chen Yajiang, Chen Ping, Li
 Jun, Li Huaxing, Wu Yang, Zhou Guiqing, Zhang
 Guanrong, Zhang Yan, Mo Wenxing, Mo Zhoubao,
 Gu Jinkun, Qin Wei, E Yi, Huang Fuwang, Yang Wangfu,
 Wen Shaoying, Feng Xiaoming, Zhu Changsheng, Xie
 Jiemin, Meng Zi and Guan Jianzhong.

桂 林 山 水

出版者 中国旅游出版社
发行者 桂林市新华书店
北 京 新 华 彩 印 厂 印 刷
1985年9月第1版 1988年3月第三次印刷
ISBN 7-5032-0129-0 / J·13
印数: 9001-16000 定价: 28元

中 华 人 民 共 和 国 印 刷
Printed in the People's Republic of China

CONTENTS

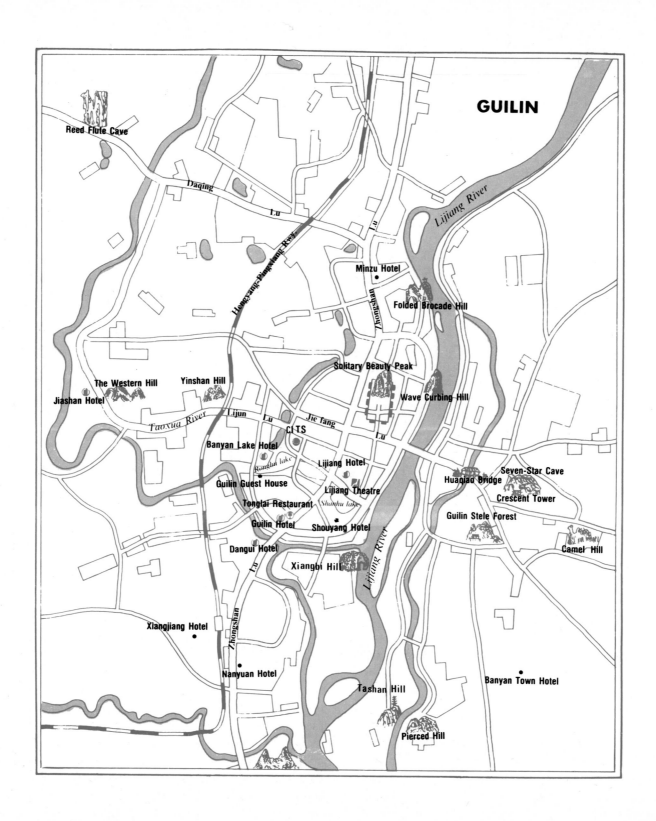

GUILIN

Reed Flute Cave

Daqing Lu

Lijiang River

Minzu Hotel

Folded Brocade Hill

Hengyang-Pingxiang Rwy

Zhongshan Lu

Solitary Beauty Peak

The Western Hill

Yinshan Hill

Wave Curbing Hill

Jiashan Hotel

Taoxua River

Lijun Lu

Jie fang

Lu

CITS

Banyan Lake Hotel

Ronghu lake

Lijiang Hotel

Huaqiao Bridge

Seven-Star Cave

Guilin Guest House

Lijiang Theatre

Crescent Tower

Tonglai Restaurant

Shanhu lake

Guilin Stele Forest

Guilin Hotel

Shouyang Hotel

Dangui Hotel

Camel Hill

Lijiang River

Xiangbi Hill

Xiangjiang Hotel

Zhongshan Lu

Nanyuan Hotel

Banyan Town Hotel

Tashan Hill

Pierced Hill

—Foreword—

Hills and Rivers in Guilin as Beautiful as Landscape Paintings

—By Liu Shou-bao

China is a land of beauty, scenery everywhere is as beautiful as a painting.

Hills and rivers in Guilin are said to be as beautiful as landscape paintings and even more beautiful than landscape paintings. Over one hundred pictures chosen in the picture album "Guilin" are just more than one hundred beautiful landscape paintings. Among them are hills and rivers, lyric sceneries, special close-ups, as well as culture and customs of the people. These extraordinary pictures will take you to the hills and rivers in Guilin, which are "unparalled" in China. As you look over this album, you will feel as if the elegant hills and rivers were right at your side, into your eyes and in your hearts.

At daybreak, as the rising sun jumps out of the horizon, its shimming rays amid patches of floating clouds fill hills and rivers in Guilin. What a bright-coloured oil painting is unfolding before us! Drizzles splash upon the tops of hills, which instantly turn luxuriant and verdent. It is just like a crystal clear water colour that will make you feel enchanting and intoxicating. During rainy seasons, the one-hundred-li Lijiang River resembles an overwhelming and rapturous Chinese ink painting, accompanying you cordially and affectionately. Whenever you stroll along Guilin's streets, parks, riverside and lakeside, there always seems as if a landscape painting were in front of you. Even the image reflected in the ripples turns out to be an elegant painting. The same hill, viewed from different angles, presents you with a different painting. You can find poems and paintings amidst hills and rivers in Guilin; that is, there are poems in the paintings and paintings in the poems. Both poems and paintings, however, can hardly be divorced from the theme, "Hills and Waters". The answer to the assessment of the hills and rivers in Guilin is probably "wonderful hills and elegant rivers".

Hills in Guilin are wonderful because they are all standing upright as if they were pulling out abruptly from the flat ground, willing to match the heaven. The craftsman, Nature, created one grotesque hill after another in Guilin after hundreds of millions of years' painstaking labour. Some are towering and precipitous, some give you a very lively feeling, bearing striking resemblance to our daily objects—like elephants, camals, horses, lions, green lotus. spring bamboo shoots, green screens or emerald hairpins;...... You can see different shapes from different hills, presenting you fantastic views everywhere.

Rivers in Guilin are interwined with hills and they embrace with each other. Rivers are indeed as elegant and charming as hills. Guilin is well-known for its "elegant" water. It is so clean that it seems transparent. It is as bright as a murcury mirror, clearly reflecting the inverted floating clouds, green trees and hills, offering a beautiful view of "all the jutting green peaks reflected on the blue water". Water in Guilin is crystal clear, flowing in a zigzag way through numerous grotesque hills; some dancing lightly; some murmuring; some singing merrily, showing the affectionate and romantic character.

People make similes, saying that grotesque hills are the frame of Guilin; flowers and trees are the skin of Guilin and water of Lijiang River is the blood of Guilin. "Hills become more lively with the contrast of water."

"Water becomes more charming with the contrast of hills." The painting of Guilin owes much to hills and rivers and the colours of the painting are readjusted with the change of the seasons. The colour-blending tray of Nature and the lustre of seasons make sceneries of Guilin full of variation and full of charm.

Hills and rivers in Guilin are really enticing and colourful.

In spring, flowers are in full bloom, breaking up the keynote of bluish-green colours. As spring rain lingers, mists prevail over numerous peaks, with a shroud of ashen and lightgreen colour and with the fading of clouds and mists, the colours are changed to verdant and bluish-purple. At the time of late spring and early summer when mixed vapour and rain prevail, you can see the peaks surrounded by drifting clouds and the green hills meandering forward like dragons.

The most alluring part in Guilin are its caverns. Out of over four hundred caverns in the city proper, the Reed Flute Cave and the Seven Star Cave are the most outstanding. Inside you can see stone pillars, stone curtains and flowers with dazzling colours. The red ones look like corals, the green ones like agates, the yellow ones like ambers and the white ones like jades. Under the light, the colours become richer, like wide span of rosy glow.

This album is the crystalization of the hard labour of a few photographers. Now they would like to dedicate to the readers the "beauty" of Guilin, which they snapped during dozens of years. However, hills and rivers in Guilin are so momentary and changeable, so charming and colourful. Who would have been able to portray them at their very best? Even the most famous painters in China's different dynasties failed to do so. Even the most talented poets also found difficulty doing so. The limited space and contents in this album have made it difficult to reflect fully this beautiful and huge world. It is our sincere hope that you might get a better understanding of this fairy place through this album. If you want to enjoy the real fun of Guilin, please spare time to visit there in person. Just like a Chinese saying goes: "Seeing is believing"

1. Thousands of Peaks amidst the Sea of Mists.

2. An agricultural landscape.

3. Xingping.

4. Mist and clouds over the Lijiang.

Guilin

Guilin, a town like a piece of green jade near the southern border, is a tourist attraction famed for picturesque mountains and placid waters. People like to link Guilin with sweet osmanthus, as its name suggests in Chinese. The city is covered in this luxuriant plant, and in autumn is heavy with its aroma. Guilin has three kinds of osmanthus, red, white and yellow.

Situated in the northeast of Guangxi Zhuang Autonomous Region and in the southwest of the Hunan-Guangxi corridor (E.Long.110 16′, N.Lat.25 15′), Guilin has an area of over 2,000 square kilometers. The Lijiang River bisects the city. The western half is a busy commercial district, and the eastern part a tourist district.

History has left groups of ancient tombs, kiln sites, buildings, stone carvings and statues carved out of stone cave walls. Representative examples are the Han Dynasty (206 B.C.-220 A.D.) tombs in the Yanshan Mountains, the Stone Tower at Mulong and Tang Dynasty (618-907) cave statues in the Western Hills, kiln ruins at Dahe and the Flowery Bridge of the Song Dynasty (960-1279), the burial ground of the Marquis of Jingjiang in the Yaoshan Mountains and the King's City of the Ming Dynasty (1368-1644). Archaeological finds at the Zengpi Cave testify that 10,000 years ago Neolithic people were living around this area.

Among the 700,000 people of Guilin 11 nationalities are represented, including the Han, Zhuang, Miao and Yao.

The area was part of an immense sea 320 million years ago. The sea bottom rose in a shift in the earth's crust called the Guangxi Movement; approximately 200 to 180 million years ago it became dry land. Later the sea returned from the southeast and the dry land was submerged under water once again. Strenuous orogenic movements eventually brought the land up a second time. Winds and rains through the eons have eroded the limestone and about one million years ago shaped the present landscape of exquisite peaks.

The mountains in Guilin are grotesque in shape, distinct from the high mountain ranges in north China that run several hundred kilometers. Guilin's long peaks rise abruptly from the ground in a multitude of forms. Duxiu Peak looks like a pillar supporting the sky; Diecai Mountain resembles piles of colorful brocade; Qixing Mountain is said to be seven stars on earth; Laoren Mountain looks like a seated old man; Xiangbi Mountain resembles an elephant drinking water with its trunk; and Luotuo Mountain resembles a camel with a heavy burden. The waters of Guilin are exquisitely clear. Lacking the imposing magnificence of the rolling Yellow and Yangtze Rivers, the Lijiang meanders quietly among the green peaks.

The karst caves in Guilin are colorful and one is never like the next. The Qixing and Ludi Caves, known as palaces of arts, have numerous changing scenes. Rocks of Guilin are unique in their own way too—translucent, smooth and delicate in shapes.

People have summarized the characteristics of Guilin's mountains and waters as "exquisite ˋpeaks, clear river water grotesque karst caves and beautiful rocks."

5. A corner of the city.

6. Crossing by the Folded Brocade Hill.
7. Morning in the market.
8. Washing melons.

9. Touring on the Lijiang.

10. Buddhist relief carvings in the Western Hills.

11. Mulong dagoba.

Folded Brocade Hill

Diecai (Folded Brocade) Hill, lying north of the city proper on the western bank of the Lijiang, earned its name from the parallel cracks that cut the hill into several layers to look like piles of embroidered brocade. It is also called Fengdong and Guishan.

Diecai Hill is composed of the Siwang Hill, Yuyue Hill, Xianhe Hill and Mingyue Peak. The Diecai Pavilion near the summit was built 100 years ago during the reign of Qing Emperor Guang Xu as a vantage point to view the hill and the whole city. Carved on the western stone wall of the pavilion are five characters: "Where the mountains and river join." Inside a mountain gate is the Yangzhi Hall in memory of Qu Shisi and Zhang Tongchang, two Ming Dynasty generals who fought against the Qing army's invasion. The hall houses the general's portraits and a poem entitled "Song of Noble Ideals" they composed in the Qing court prison. Two poems by Guo Moruo are carved below the portraits in tribute.

Several dozen steps upward lead to "Wind Cave", where a cool breeze blows the year round. There are more than 90 Buddhist statues of various sizes carved out of the cave walls, works between 700 and 1,000 years old. On display in the cave are "Note on Diecai Hill" by Tang poet Yuan Hui, a poem by Qing poet Yuan Mei eulogizing the cave, a painting of orchards and bamboo by Qing painter Li Bingshou, a prose article by Kang Youwei from the late Qing Dynasty, and a carved portrait and a paean of contemporary patriot Ma Xiangbo.

On top of Mingyue (Bright-Moon) Peak is the Nayun Pavilion where one can enjoy a view of the city.

12. Wind Cave, Folded Brocade Hill.

13. Distant view of Folded Brocade Hill.

Wave Curbing Hill

Fubo Mountain resembles a huge stone pillar thrusting skyward by the Lijiang, and rising silightly to the north of the city proper. Many folk tales have been made up around the curiously-shaped mountain. One legend says that Ma Yuan, who had the title of General Fubo in the Han Dynasty (206 B.C.-220 A.D.) shot arrows from the summit and hit three other mountains. Hence the name. At the foot of the mountain near the water is the Huanzhu (Returning-the-Pearl) Cave. One story tells of a dragon who used to come to the cave to play with a pearl. One day it fell asleep, and a fishing boy took the pearl. Recognizing his misbehavior, the boy returned the pearl to the dragon. In praise of his honesty, people called the cave Huanzhu. Within, a stalactite hangs from the ceiling only two inches short of the ground. It is said this was cut by General Fubo so its name is "the rock that tried the sword."

There are more than 100 pieces of historical stone inscription and 250 statues carved in the wall, mostly works of the Tang and Song dynasties. The best include a self-portrait of Mi Fu, a famous painter of the Song Dynasty, and the "Banquet Poem" of the famous Song poet Fan Chengda. One Buddhist statue is more than 1,000 years old, and stands as an important relic for study of the relation between Chinese and Indian Buddhism.

A gigantic iron cauldron weighing 2,500 kilograms stands at the entrance to the cave, cast 300 years ago in the eighth year of Qing Emperor Kang Xi.

14. Wave Curbing Hill.

15. Self-portrait of Mi Fu. (stone carving)
16. Buddhist works in Pearl-returning Cave.
17. A Qing Dynasty iron bell.

Solitary Beauty Peak

Duxiu (Solitary-Beauty) Peak soars proudly in the King's City in the center of Guilin. Viewed from the front the peak appears precipitous; sidewise it is delicate and dignified.

Yan Yanzhi, a writer of the Southern Dynasty 1,500 years ago, described Duxiu Peak in a poem: "The sole beauty stands amidst lofty peaks." In the morning glow and at sunset Duxiu Peak is said to shine as if putting on a purple robe and a golden belt, thus its other name: "Purple and Golden Mountain."

The square King's City is a half kilometer long and one-fourth kilometer wide with a city wall running 1.5 kilometers. Construction of the city began in the early 13th century and was finished more than 20 years later. The original structures—the main hall, palace, ancestral shrine and prayer terrace, as well as 40-some pavilions and towers—were all destroyed in wars. Only the base of the city wall, some carved balustrades and steps have survived.

During the Tang Dynasty a school was built at the foot of Duxiu Peak. During the Song Dynasty, Tiezhong Temple was built and was renamed Dayuan in the Yuan Dynasty. In the Ming Dynasty, Marquis Jingjiang built a mansion here, which was converted into a scholar's academy in the Qing Dynasty. At the beginning of the Republic of China Sun Yat-sen had his headquarters here for a time. There are also scenic spots—the Reading Rock, Peaceful Rock and Crescent Moon Pool. Steps on the west lead up the peak to the Southern Heavenly Gate.

18. King's city.

19. Solitary Beauty Peak. 27

Reed Flute Cave

Ludi (Reed-Flute) Cave is hidden deep in the Guangming Mountain in the northwestern part of Guilin, seven kilometers from the center of the city. Its name comes from the fact that the species of reed growing by the cave entrance can be made into sweet-sounding pipes. The horseshoe-shaped cave is 240 meters deep. Numerous stalactites, stalagmites, stone columns and stone flowers form strange scenes.

20. Outdoor scene at Reed Flute Cave.

21. Reed Flute
    Cave interior.

Seven-Star Park

The Qixing (Seven-Stars) Park, two kilometres from the city center on the eastern bank of the Lijiang, is the largest and most beautiful park in Guilin. Qixing Mountain and Qixing Cave are located in its 40 hectares.

Qixing Mountain, in the center of the park, is composed of Mt. Putuo and three peaks of Yueya Mountain. The Lingjian and the Xiaodong Rivers flow among the peaks. A decorated bridge crosses a river at the entrance to the west gate. A collection of stone tablets is hidden in the rocks close to the south gate. Luotuo (Camel) Hill stands to the east. Flanking Luotuo Hill are a miniature landscape garden and a zoo. On a little island north of the decorated bridge and at the confluence of the two rivers is a children's playground.

The Qixing Cave hides deep within Mt. Putuo, on which monks' living quarters, the Jinjiang Tower, the Yueya Tower, the Zhaixing Pavilion and the Lanyue Pavilion fit beautifully into the scenery. These scenic spots are all connected by winding paths.

Qixing Cave is a labyrinth underground. Colorful stalactites, stalagmites, stone screens and stone flowers fill the 800-meter-long cave to form over 40 gorgeous scenes with poetic names such as ''Banyan Tree Greeting Guests'', ''Frontier Village'', ''A Gathering of Heroes'', ''Magpie-Bridge over Milky Way'', ''Peacock Spreading Tail'' and ''Offering Peaches to Guests''. One vivid scene depicts Chang'E, the immortal girl in the moon, dancing under an osmanthus tree; another the two lovers -- the cowherd and weaving girl -- looking longingly at each other over the Milky Way; a third portrays Nuwa, the creator of man in Chinese legend, melting stones to patch up a leaking spot in the sky.

22. Flowery Bridge.

23. Camel Hill.

24. Dragon Refuge Crag.
25. Tortoise and snake in one ——an ancient art work.
26. Mount Putuo.

27. Pearl curtain
inside Seven-
Star Cave.

29

Potted Landscape

An exquisite garden beside Luotuo Hill has an array of more than 1,000 potted miniature landscapes in various sizes. Those displayed in the front hall are miniature hills placed in pots of water, and those in the rear hall are made of stalagmites and stalactites. In between the two halls are a pond, a delicate bridge, a flower nursery and pavilions linked by corridors.

Arenaceous rocks are collected from the river bottom below the Water-falls along the Lijiang. These stones and pieces of petrified wood are carefully carved and grafted to form graceful miniature landscapes. Then evergreen grass and tiny trees are planted and towers and pavilions erected to recreate miniature scenes from Guilin. Landscapes made of stalagmites and stalactites are further beautified with a decorative tray to give a feeling of antiquity.

28. Karst golden-fish pot.
29. Stalactite potted landscapes.

South Stream Hill

Nanxi Mountain, renowned as "first among the famous mountains of Guilin", stands in the southern part of the metropolis. The Lijiang runs to its east and the Nanxi River meanders around its foot. The single-arch double-curve Jinlian (Golden-Lotus-Flower) Bridge spans the river and a pavilion in ancient style on the bridge affords a scenic view. South of the bridge is the crystalline Bailong (White-Dragon) Fountain. A legend has it that the water of the fountain was reserved for emperors to make tea, thus another name "Tribute Fountain". Within Nanxi Mountain are Bailong Cave, Xuanyan Cave Longji Cave and Liuxian Cave, in which stalagmites and stalactites display dazzling forms and colors. Bailong, Xuanyan and Longji caves are connected by tunnels to help tourists.

30. Longji Pavilion on South Stream Hill.

Banyan Lake, Fir Lake

These two lakes are like crystal pieces inlaid in the center of the city. Originally a part of the moat before the city expanded southward, the lakes are divided by a Song Dynasty Bridge and now are part of the inner city. The eastern one is called Shan (Fir) Lake because fir trees once grew on its bank, and the western part called Rong (Banyan) Lake because there is a banyan tree near the water in front of the old south gate. Today bamboo, willows, peaches and osmanthus on the bank enhance the beauty of the two lakes. An islet in the middle of Rong Lake has a pavilion with yellow windows, silvery pillars, pink walls and green glazed tiles to balance the south gate tower over a distance. On an islet in Shan Lake are a round tower and four pavilions in the shape of mushrooms. Artistically arranged in height and distance, these structures, curving lake banks, a bow-shaped corridor and moon-shaped seats form a round cluster. By the lakes are the Ronghu and Lijiang hotels.

31. A thousand-year old banyan tree.

32. Fir Lake.

Zengpi Cave

Nine kilometers south of Guilin proper, at the foot of Dushan Mountain, Zengpi Cave is an archaeological site of the New Stone Age. Excavation formally began in 1973, and many artifacts of stone, bone, shell and pottery were found. Stone utensils made either by carving or grinding—adzes, axes, chisels and spears—are in greater number. Bone articles include awls, arrowheads, needles and hairpins. Shell articles include spades, knives, ladles and ornaments. There are pottery jars and stemmed cups and bowls. The middle area on the cave served as a fire pit for heating, cooking and baking pottery as well as a meeting place of elders. More than 30 skeletons of all sexes and ages have been exhumed around an ash pit near the fire pit. Archaeologists found a mother and son buried together, group burials of close relatives and a particular burial form in which the dead were squatting.

Another find was the Lijiang Deer, of medium size and graceful body—the first of its kind ever discovered in China.

The finds at the Zengpi Cave show that the place was inhabited about 10,000 years ago, and have filled up a blank space in research on the New Stone Age in southern China.

33. Burial objects in the deep cave. (painting)

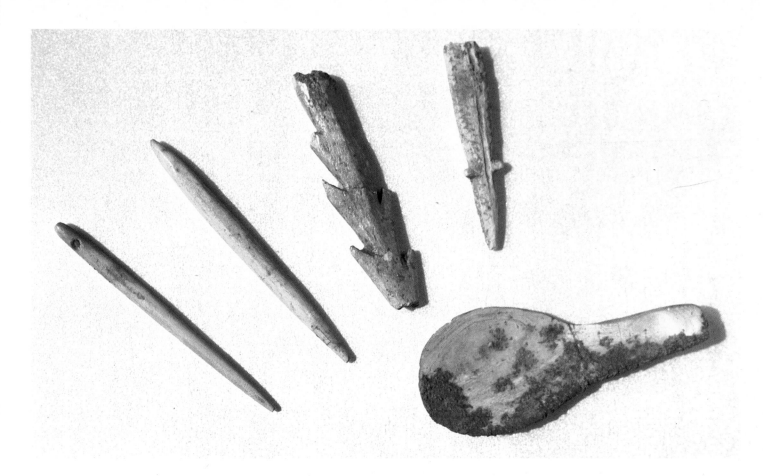

34. Bone needles, fish fork, spear and clam spoon unearthed from Zengpi ruins.

35. Calligrapher and seal carver-Li Luogong.

36. Carved inscription by Professor Li Luogong.

Guilin stele forest

There are nearly 2,000 inscriptions relating to politics, history, economy, culture, city construction, science and the art of calligraphy carved on cave walls. Longyin Cave at the foot of Yaoguang Peak of Qixing Mountain has the most. In 1963 the State Cultural Relics Administration built a stone inscription repository outside the entrance to store rubbings. The repository and cave are known as the "Tablet Forest of Guilin".

Among the most important inscriptions are "Records of the Factions During the Year of Yuanyou" reflecting the inner struggles of parties in the Song Dynasty ruling class. The inscription "On the Five Evils" expounds five malpractices in official circles, exposing in metaphor the bribery, corruption, extravagance and lawless activities of the officials.

A map carved on a stone wall shows the layout of the city and military establishments of Guilin in the Southern Song Dynasty, a rare example of such large scale, rich content and early date in China so far.

The handwriting of Guilin stone inscriptions was done in all five calligraphic styles of xing, zhen, zhuan, cao and li. The name plaque of the Carefree Tower by Tang calligrapher Yan Zhenqing and a title of a prose article by Shi Manqing of the Song Dynasty have been used as models through generations. Inscriptions written by Song Dynasty calligraphers Mi Fu and Huang Tingjian, powerful and smooth, are master works of the xing style. Titles and inscriptions of Tang Dynasty Li Yangbing and Song Dynasty Zeng Bu in zhuan style appear archaic and unsophisticated. "Notes of Diecai Hill" done by Yuan Hui of the Tang Dynasty, and the "Song of Welcoming and Seeing Off Gueste" are rare pieces of li style calligraphy.

37. Guilin Stele Forest.

Old south gate

The Old South Gate is on the northern bank of Rong Lake in Guilin. Said to be more than 1,300 years old, it still stands solidly. The gate is attended by a banyan tree also more than 1,000 years old. A legend says that in the period of Wude (618-627) under the reign of Tang Emperor Gao Zu, a famous general (Li Jing) was garrison commander of Guilin and built this gate. In later dynasties the city expanded to the edge of the Taohua River and the former gate became known as Old South Gate. The gate tower is of red pillars and blue glazed tiles. In 1963 Guo Moruo wrote a name plaque which hangs on the southern side of the gateway.

38. Old South Gate.

Wild Goose Hill Park

Yanshan Park at Yangshuo, 22 kilometers from Guilin, was built in 1869 as a private garden of Tang Zishi. On an area of 70 hectares, structures of ancient style are enhanced by natural waters and hills, characteristic of landscapes of southern China.

A Pair of clear ponds with lotus flowers flank the entrance of the park. Fangzhu Hill and Zhongru Hill stand symmetrically on the northern and southern ends. The Xiangsi River flows through the park. Xiangsi Cave, Biyun Lake, Daoxiang Village, the Hongdou Courtyard, the Linlang Mansion, Huashen Lake, Chengyan Hall and the Hantong Tower decorate the park amidst rare plants such as green-stemmed plum and jequirity trees.

39. Wild Goose Hill Park.

40. On the Peach Blossom River.
41. Kinds of essence made of osmanthus.
42. Osmanthus (red)
43. Osmanthus (white)

The Lijiang River

LIJIANG

Xiangbi Hill
Douji Hill
Guilin
Tashan Hill
Chuanshan Hill
Jingping Hill
Zhemu
Guilin Airport
Longmencun
Qifengzhen
Daxu
Mopan Hill
Lijiang River
Liangfeng
Jiuniu Ridge
Yanshan
Biya Hill
Mingcun
Wangfu Rock
Caopingxu
Crown Cave
Strange Half-Side Ferry
Xiushan Hill
Taoyuan
Celestial Being Turning Millstone
Yangdi
Langshi
Huashan Hill
Huanghu Sands
Luosi Hill
Xingping
Yu cun
Baisha
Pubutang
Yangmei Ping
Yangshuo
Aged Banyan Tree
Fuli
Yueliang Hill   Bilian Peak   Shutong Hill

Flowing from the Mao'er Mountains in Xing'an County northeast of Guilin, the Lijiang traverses a zigzag route of 437 kilometres through many valleys southeastward in Guilin, Yangshuo, Pingle and Zhaoping counties to join the Xijiang River at Wulin. The most beautiful section of the Lijiang is a length of 83 kilometres from Guilin to Yangshuo that abounds with picturesque peaks, waterfalls, woods, rare plants and clusters of farm houses.

Riding in a boat from Guilin, one sees Shuiyue Cave and Yueyan Cave in Xiangbi and Chuan hills. These two caves, open at both ends, look like a pair of mirrors: one floating on the emerald water and the other inlaid in the sky. They are said to be a pair of wise eyes that reflect the beauty and purity of the Lijiang. Downstream are the vivid shape of Xiangbi Hill, Douji Mountain, which resembles a fighting cock, and Jingping Mountain in the shape of a long-necked water jar.

The river water is green and crystalline, reflecting the numerous peaks along the banks. The river bottom is visible. Two lines of a poem describe the scene: "Green Mountaintops are distinguishable. The boat rides atop the mountains."

It is fascinating to watch fishing on the Lijiang. Slim bamboo rafts speed on the water surface like shuttles, and each raft carries four or five fish hawks. The fishermen sing and hoot the birds into the water; they dive and soon reappear with half-swallowed fish. In autumn, the banks are bright with golden persimmons, pomeloes and tangerines.

The most interesting element in enjoying a trip to Lijiang is seeing Mural Hill, a sheer cliff rising abruptly out of the water. The face of the hill is variegated and has on it the extraordinary likenesses of nine horses, all in different positions, and all formed by nature, in the lines and streaks on the rock face.

45

46

47. Summer on
the Lijiang.

49. Returning boat.

48. Clear Water.

50. Rafts.
51. Boat on clear water.

52. Spring on the Lijiang.

53. Zhupi Shoal.

54. Sending vegetables to Guilin.
55. Swimming.
56. Visiting parents.

57. Raft reflection.
58. Sail's reflection on the waves.

59. Cooking fish.

60 Rosy dawn.

61. Earthly Fairyland.

62. Elephant Trunk Hill.

Elephant Trunk Hill

Located at the confluence of the Lijiang and the Taohuajiang inside the city of Guilin, the hill vividly resembles an elephant sucking water from the river with its trunk. The image of the elephant's trunk, eyes, body and tail is perfectly clear. Between the trunk and legs of the elephant is a round-shaped space, known as "water moon arch". On the back of the elephant is a brick-pagoda shaped octagon.

Elephant Trunk Hill is regarded as the symbol of Guilin, and is used as the trade mark for most commodity products made in the city.

Pierced Hill

This name derives from a cave which pierces the hill from north to south. The cave looks very peculiar, like a bright mirror or a full moon. Hence the name: "Empty Bright Cave", also known as "moon rock cave". Viewed from afar, Pierced-Through Hill looks like a beacon illuminating the ancient city of Guilin.

Pierced-Through Hill joins with its neighbouring Tashan Hill and the Pierced-Through Hill Rock at its foot to form the Pierced-Through Hill Park. In the Pierced-Through Hill Rock is a newly-discovered karst cave with a length of 500 metres. Inside the cave, numerous crystalline rocks decorate the surface of the stalactites with fantastic shapes like tree branches; and tapering crystalizations called "crystal needles" and "stone branches". In addition, some hang from the ceiling, like glass tubes as large as chopsticks, called "goose tubes". All of these stalactites are rarely seen in the Reed Flute Cave or the Seven Star Rock.

63. At the foot of Pierced Hill.

64. Marvellous Spectacle of Grotto.

Town of Strange Pinnacles

If you fly to Guilin, you will find nemerous grotesque peaks soaring into the sky as you land at the airport. Indeed, people are amazed by the natural scene. If you take a pleasure-boat along the Lijiang, you will enjoy another sight as the boat reaches the area around the Zhemu Township: numerous peaks standing tall and straight, majestic and beautiful along the river, as if emerging from the water. Looking carefully, you will find blue peaks in the distance, as if hanging on the edge of the sky while nearer peaks look like soft green bamboo shoots. The magnificent view attracts many poets and painters.

65. Hill of Wonderful Peak.

66. The drillground of Hong Xiuquan.

68. A Peasant's Family.

67. Mist over Strange Pinnacles.

Daxu
(The Country Fair)

Daxu has been one of the four big country fairs in Guangxi since the Ming Dynasty (1368-1644).

Built with blue stone, the town's main street stretches 2.5 kilometres from north to south. On both sides of the street stand many buildings with blue bricks and tiles, decorated with paintings in local style. At the north end of the town lies the Gao Zu Temple, Han Emperors' Temple, Hunan Guild Hall and Guangdong Guild Hall, at its south end lies theLongevity Bridge with a single rainbow-shaped arch. The bridge was built about 400 years ago. The countryside fair is now held once every three days and on the fair day, the street is bustling with activity. Village women and mountain peasants are in high spirits, coming to sell their agricultural and sideline products, and then buying salt and other daily necessities.

69. Basking in the Sun Shine.

70. Fishing Fire.

Crown Cliff

Situated 15 kilometres south of Guilin, the cavern bears a strong resemblance to an ancient golden crown. Hence the name of Crown Cavern. Inside the cave, there is a limpid stream of 10 kilometres, which flows slowly into the Lijiang One may sail a special-made bamboo raft upstream to the cave. There are four grottoes in the cavern, each one uniquely different. The stalactites inside the grottoes are grotesque and diversified, forming a fantastic crystal palace. Ancients admired the cave as much as the marvellous waters and mountains.

71. Fishermen at rest.

72. Crown Cliff.

Yangdi Village

The name "Yangdi" came from the fact that there lies a mountain with two peaks shaped like sheep hooves behind Yangdi (literally the sheep Embankment) Village. Sheep hooves are pronounced "yang ti" in Chinese, and people use a homophonic term "Yang Di" to name the village. During the dry season, Yangdi is the dock where pleasure-boats start down the Lijiang. The landscape here is the finest among the scenic spots along the Lijiang, including the wonders of the "Gold chicken pecking at rice", "Three old men gathering" and "Carp hanging on the wall".

73. Snow.

74. Riverboats at Yangdi.

Spindrift Stone

In the river beside the Spindrift Stone Village, there are many broken rocks, which look like undulating spindrifts, hence the name. As pleasure-boats pass through the Spindrift Stones, arrays of hills and peaks stand along both banks as if to welcome and see their guests off. On the right bank of the river stand the Greater Yellow Hill, Penholder Hill, Literal Pen Hill and Soaring-to-the-Sky Hill; on the left bank are White Rabbit Hill, Egg Hill, Phoenix Hill and Avalokitesvara Hill, forming a gorge, in the middle of which is a round rock called "Apple Rock".

75. Autumn.

76. Spindrift Stone scenery.

Mural Hill

On the cruise down the Lijiang, 61 kilometres from Guilin, a stone hill stands on the left bank. On the huge multi-coloured cliff are interwoven colours of blue, yellow, green and white; some are rich and gaudy, others are elegant, making the hill a colossal "mural", hence the name. Images of horses in various postures, some of them jumping and galloping, others grazing and sleeping, seem to have been painted by some enormous hand. According to a legend, these horses were spirit horses in heaven, attracted by the sight of the Lijiang. As they were rolling, jumping, galloping and grazing on the grass, they were startled by a painter who approached them and wished to depict them. Immediately, the horses ran towards the hill and merged into the cliff. Thousands of tourists are now attracted by the images of Nine-Horse Mural Hill. They stand in front of the hill and search out the images of the horses. A folk rhyme refering to the imperial examinations says, "Your name will be on the list of the successful candidates if you can recognize seven horses, and you will become the number one scholar if you can find nine horses".

77. Nine-horse Mural Hill.

Huangbu Shoal

Yellow Cloth Shoal is an excellent place for watching the inverted reflections in the Lijiang. On the banks of Yellow Cloth Shoal stand seven peaks of different sizes, as if rising from the water. These peaks are tall and erect, resembling seven maidens. A legend has it that seven pretty fairies descended to the world from heaven and were so attracted by the landscape that they forgot to return. The Jade Emperor learned of this and called them back, but they were so infatuated with the sight of the Lijiang that they preferred to stay in the world, and changed themselves into stone peaks by blowing a supernatural chilling wind.

Weather has an important bearing on watching the inverted reflection. Rain and fog both destroy the effect; only on a fine day can the inverted images be seen clearly.

78. Huangbu shoal.

Situated in the northern part of Yangshuo County, Xing Ping has observed several spectacular landscapes for over 1,300 years. Some of the peaks are named "Maiden looks in the mirror", "General draws his sword", "God of longevity mounts deer", "Carp swallows water", "Tablet pierces the sky" (meaning a tablet held before the breast by officials when received in audience by the emperor) and "Spiral sleeps in the river". All these peaks, together with green bamboo and bending willows and cottages on both banks sometimes can be seen invert in the water.

Xingping

79. Night in Xinping,

80. A thousand year-old town.

81. Dawn mist over Xingping.

69

82. Chaoban Hill.

A Happy Fishing Family

A fisherman is happy for having three treasures —bamboo raft, fishing net and cormorants.

A bamboo raft is made of five bamboos by lashing them together. The large end in called the raft stem. The simple and swift bamboo raft provides economical shallow-draft transportation for fishermen.

Fishing nets are of several types: floating nets, sinking nets, casting nets and stake nets, each used according to the streamflow and depth of water as well as the strategy for catching various kinds of fish.

Cormorants have been in fishing for over 1,000 years in China. A good cormorant can catch as many fish as three intelligent and capable fishermen.

Cormorants lay four or five eggs in January or February each year. If a cormorant is bred well, it will lay more eggs the same size as duck eggs. Chicken hens incubate the eggs instead of cormorants because cormorants have no role in hatching their eggs. Usually it takes 40-50 days to hatch cormorant eggs. The young cormorant can not open its eyes for seven days after it hatches. On the eighth day, fine soft down grown on its body; only after 100 days can a cormorant be said to be full-fledged.

As soon as a cormorant becomes full-fledged in the fourth month, it can live independently and go into the river to catch fish to fill its own stomach. When two years old, it may become a "labourer" for fisherman. The adult cormorant is full of vigour; richly experienced, a five-year-old can catch fish independently or together with four or five fellows. A good cormorant can catch 50 kg. of fish a day; sometimes a fish the cormorant catches is more than 5 kg. If one cormorant can not land a big fish, the other two or three immediately come and help it draw the fish out of the water.

Each time, cormorants are rewarded by fisherman as soon as the fishing is over. The fisherman unfastens a swallowing-preventive collar tied around the cormorant's neck, then gives it small fish or shrimp.

Sometimes, fishermen go out and fish at night. They take three or five bamboo rafts together with a dozen cormorants to a river or a lake. Hanging a gas lamp on the bamboo rafts, the fishermen step down and up the rafts and shout in order to force their cormorants into the river. The cormorants swim back and forth, seizing fish out of the water.

86. Evening glow.

87. Winner.
88. Cormorant.
89. Capture.

73

90. A Fishing Village.

Misty Rain on the Lijiang

The Lijiang is unquestionably very beautiful on a fine day, but it is also charming in misty rain. Peaks and hills look like young ladies who cover their beautiful faces with thin veils. Sometimes the fog curtain lifts and mountains appear shyly from the swirling clouds and mist. Misty rain gives Lijiang a dynamic feature; just as a Chinese proverb goes, "The Lijiang is mysterious in blurred misty rain and dynamic with change."

91. Wild Crossing.

Green Bamboo
by the Lijiang

Including golden bamboo, pheonix-tail bamboo and Bodhisattva bamboo, bamboo grows along the Lijiang from the ancient town of Daxu to Yangshuo, extending more than a dozen kilometres and forming a green wall. It serves as a foil to the green water of the Lijiang reenforcing a quiet and beautiful green world.

People living along both banks of Lijiang River like, plant, and make use of bamboo. They have a bond with the bamboo and they make various types of furniture with bamboo, chairs, beds, baskets, curtains; even when they go fishing, they use the bamboo rafts and bamboo punt-poles. Sometimes, they blow bamboo flutes. Bamboo is inseparable from the Lijiang, and the local people are inseparable from bamboo.

93. Fishing Boats on Lijiang River.　　　　**92. Pushing out of the earth.**

94. Quiet and beautiful.
95. Return from Herding.

77

Yangshuo

Situated 65 kilometres southeast of Guilin, Yangshuo is a county under the jurisdiction of the city of Guilin. In the north of the county is Yangjiao Hill (meaning "sheep's horn"), hence the name Yangshuo.

Yangshuo is an ancient town, whose past can be traced back to the Jin Dynasty (265-420) when the county seat was moved here from Xingping. Surrounded by the Lijiang and the Tianjiahe River, Yangshuo County embraces 12 rivers, large and small, so it is called "river town" and, also known as "mountain town" for it is bounded by Longtou (Dragon Head) Hill, Duli Hill, Yangjiao (Sheep Horn) Hill, Tian'e (Swan) Hill, Tianma (Heaven Horse) Hill, Ma'an (Horse Saddle) Hill and Green Lotus Peak. An ancient Chinese traveller, Xu Xiake once praised it as the "world of green lotus and jade bamboo shoot". Yangshuo won its fame for its green hills, charming waters, peculiar peaks and exquisite caverns. In addition to Shutong (scholar's page-boy) Hill, Beautiful Maiden Hill, God of Longevity Hill and Little Cat Hill, there stands Moon Hill, inside which one finds Anji Cave runing from bottom to top. Yangshuo is a beautiful place with green hills and clear waters, famed for its rich local produce, such as sweet oranges and tangerines.shaddock, persimmons, Chinese chestnuts and kumquats.

96. Stone inscription.
97. Late spring in the hill town.

98. Rosy dawn over Dongling in fog.

99. Boats floating a top green hills.

100. Scholar's Page-Boy Hill.

101. Angling Terrace.

102. East Youth Hill.

103. Picturesque Scene in a mountain village.

83

Green Lotus Peak

Situated on the west bank of the Lijiang and connecting with the county site of Yangshuo in the east, the peak owes its name to its shape, which resembles a budding green lotus. A scenic path halfway up the peak is provided so tourists can get a panoramic view of the Ancient Banyan Peak, Phoenix Mountain, the God of Longevity Peak, Chibi Peak and Donghua Peak in the distance; nearby, tourists can also enjoy figures and inscriptions carved on the slope of the peak cliff. Among these are the poems titled "Households live among the Green Lotus Peak" written by Shen Bin in the Tang Dynasty (618-907) and "The peak is rarely seen" written by Li Gang, prime minister in the Song Dynasty (960-1279) and the poem "Guilin, a city that leads the world in beauty, and Yangshuo even more beautiful than Guilin" by Wu Mai, a patriotic writer of modern times. In addition, the character "dai" (meaning region) was written by Wang Yuanren, a Qing Dynasty calligrapher, in a vivid and vigorous style, urging young people to work hard. At the north end of the path stands the Riverside Pavilion and the Mirror Hill Pavilion.

104. Riverside Pavilion.

105. The character "Dai", three metres high, carved on a hill cliff, urging young people to work hard.

Yangshuo Park

Yangshuo Park, in the city of Yangshuo, is surrounded by hills and peaks, with a ribbon-like creek running through it. Solitary Beauty Hill, Xilang hill and Zhongling Hill stand majestically in the park. On their summits are "Let-Go-the-Crane Pavilion", "Meet-the-Immortals Pavilion" and "Reposing-on-the-Clouds Pavilion".

107. West Youth Hill.

Pierced Rock

Situated by the Pierced-Through Rock Village, 7 Kilometres south of Yangshuo, this rock owes its name to a cave piercing through a small stone outcropping. The Jinbao River runs swiftly past the rock, and on the opposite bank grows an ancient massive banyan tree. Standing by the banyan tree one can view the "Gold Hook Rock", the "Frog Rock" on the Jinbao River and the "Petty Bear Rock" halfway up the hill in the south. Pierced-Through Rock and the neighbouring hills, such as the Shuizha, Wuzhi and Fenglou are connected to each other by the Qinge Ferry nearby, forming a rural landscape with unique style.

108. Village Customs.

109. Ancient banyan at Qing'e.
110. Rosy clouds over green peaks.

111. Dawn and Dusk

A Street in Yangshuo

Arranged in a "S" and surrounded by hills and peaks, the street of Yangshuo is a small urban street no more than a kilometre long, along which stand buildings with two or four stories. Shops and department stores are arranged one after the other on both sides of the street. A Friendship Store, cultural relics shop, arts and crafts shop, tourist goods shop, department store, Chinese painting and calligraphy shop as well as fruit shop, cigarettes and wine shop, daily necessities store, family-use electrical equipment store and restaurants compose the town. With great varieties, these shops sell pearls and jewels, jadeite and agate, cultural relics, stone carving, jade, bamboo, wood and ivory, metal arts of gold, silver and copper as well as the "four treasures of the study" (writing brush, ink stick, ink slab and paper). In addition, mountains-and-waters of Guilin paintings and souvenirs are available.

112. A Street in Yangshuo.

113. A pyramid-shaped dumpling made of glutinous rice wrapped in bamboo or reed leaves.

114. Glutinous rice cake.

115. Shatian pomelos.
116. Antique shop.
117. Returning from a
     rewarding journey.

118. Buying Chinese herbal medicines.

119. Kumquats.

Red-clay Pottery in Yangshuo

Red-clay pottery is a fine pottery without glaze made by firing at high temperature. The pottery is prepared and manufactured meticulously by Zhou Qingli, an arts engineer. With a bright and ruddy colour, it has close texture and high gloss. The products of tea pot, jar, cup and tripod made in the Chenguan Pottery and Pocelain Factory in Yangshuo are well received by tourists both at home and abroad.

120. Red-clay pottery in Yangshuo.

Ling Canal at Xing'an

In Xing'an County, 65 kilometres south of Guilin, is the ancient Ling canal, built about 2,000 years ago.

In ancient times, the Xiangjiang (part of the Yangtze River) and the Lijiang (a tributary of the Pearl River) ran parallel, 30 kilometres apart. When the two rivers flowed into Xing'an County, the distance between the two narrowed, but they could not be connected. One flowed northward and joined the Yangtze while the other flowed southward and joined the Pearl River, pouring respectively into the East China Sea and South China Sea.

To unify South China, Emperor Qin Shi Huang (259-210 B.C.) dispatched Shi Lu to supervise the construction of the Ling Canal in 214 B.C. to connect the Xiangjiang and Lijiang. After repeated survey and investigation, a lowest and narrowest area of the watershed of the Lijiang and Xiangjiang rivers was found, where the 34-kilometre long canal was dug from north to south by cutting through the Taishi Temple Hill. The canal led water from Xiangjiang River to the Lijiang River.

In order to distribute the water from the Xiangjiang rationally and drain floods properly, supplementary projects, such as the Huazui, the Larger and Smaller Tianping, the Tianping Outlets, sluice gates and the Qin Dyke were constructed one after another following completion of the north-south canal. The Ling Canal took four years to build, but heralded other artificial canals in China.

Although advanced land transportation today has replaced boat navigation in the Ling Canal, it can not be neglected in the sustenance of agriculture, as it irrigates 30,000 mu of farmland.

121. Flood control dam.

Since construction of the Ling Canal, dredging and reconstructions have never stopped. At present, the Four-Prominent Personages Temple and the Three-Generals Tomb still stand in Xingan Park as memorials to those who made contributions to the construction of the Ling Canal. The Four-Prominent Personages Temple is to memorialize Shi Lu, Ma Yuan, Li Po and Yu Mengwei. The Three-General Tomb commemorates the generals of Zhang, Liu, and Li. It is said that the generals of Zhang and Liu were killed for not completing the Ling Canal on time. Drawing a lesson from Generals Zhang and Liu, General Li killed himself soon after completion of the canal.

122. The main irrigation ditch of Ling Canal.

123. Tourists inspect a stone dam built over 2,000 years ago.

124. The stone tablet at the confluence of the Xiangjiang and the Lijiang rivers.

Dragon-boat race at the source of the Lijiang

For 2,000 years, the dragon-boat race has been a folk activity to mourn the great poet, Qu Yuan (about 340 B.C.-278 B.C.). Nowadays, the dragon-boat race is held annually (May 5-15). Both banks of the Rongjiang River are a sea of people moving to the deafening sound of gongs and drums.

Dragon-boats come one after the other in the morning; each boat has 20 sailors who wrap their heads in white towels and neatly dress in the same colour (red, blue, white or green). The dragon-boat also has a banner-bearer, a gong player and a drum player, a helmsman and two *suona* blowers. The banner-bearer is the commander while the players of gong and drum unify the operation through their rhythms. When the dragon-boats come, boatmen sing the Melody of the Dragon-Boat and greet each other. Usually, a grand memorial ceremony is held to the sound of firecrackers and gong and drum before the race starts. As soon as the ceremony is over, the dragon-boat race begins.

125. Offering a sacrifice to dragon heads.

126. Dragon-boat race at the source of the Lijiang.

Sightseeing and Native Product

127. Jin village, Longsheng county.
128. Drying grain seeds.

129. A funeral of the Zhuang nationality.

130. Longsheng terraced fields.

131. Old friends share a laugh.

132. Fishing season.

133. Narrow mountain path.

134. Girls of Zhuang Nationality.
135. A Lass.

136. Stage photo of an opera ''Third Sister Liu''.
137. Girls of Yao Nationality.
138. A Miao girl.

139. Harvesting mangosteens.
140. A big red happiness symbol. (paper cuts)
141. Newlywed couple toasting each other.
142. Wedding.

143. A Guilin specialty--dried bean milk cream in tight rolls.

144. Water chestnuts.

145. Fermented bean curd.

146. Antique china

147. Making bowl cakes.

148. Foreigners doing shopping.
149. Eating Rice Noodle.
150. Drying cured meat.

Hotels and
Restaurants

Hotels and Guest Houses in Guilin are diversified in forms and varied in the general layout. With their unique architectural forms and rich national styles, the hotels there offer varieties of selection for the tourists. Rong Hu Hotel is a hotel with the blending of both Chinese and western architectural forms. Li Jiang Hotel is a high-rise hotel with western architectural style. Jia Shan Hotel is a courtyard-styled tourist hotel. Rong Chen Hotel is a hotel with architecture of Chinese national style. Yang Suo Hotel is a cottage and villa-styled hotel. Dan Gui Hotel and Yin Shan Hotel are both of specific characteristics, affording excellent accomodations for the guests. In addition, Gui Qing Hotel and Gui Yuan Hotel, the tourist centre, being prepared for construction, will emerge before the tourists with their unique architectural style. These hotels are located along the areas of beautiful scenery respectively. Some are built among green lotus or jade bamboo shoots. Some are situated in the vicinity of areas of beautiful scenery; some in the business centres; some in the borders of downtowns. They are located either by hills and rivers or surrounded by hills and facing lakes or by the slopes and along the rivers. These hotels and guest houses correspond harmoniously with the hills and rivers of Guilin, thus adding charm and lustre to Guilin.

151. Night view of Li Jiang Hotel.

152. Banyan Town Hotel.

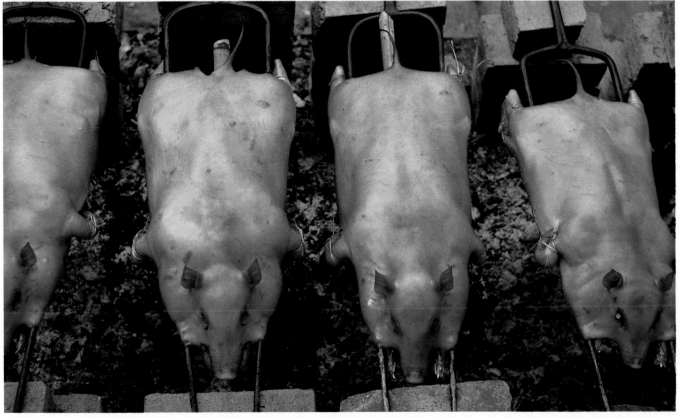

153. Suckling pigs roasting.

105

160. Banquet Hall of
     Banyan Lake Hotel.
161. Bar in the Jia Shan
     Hotel.

Love